Verses from the Plains

A Poetry Collection

Compiled by
Nebraska Writers Guild

NWG Publications
Scottsbluff, NE

Copyright © 2020 NWG Publications

All rights reserved. No part of this publication may be used or reproduced in any manner without prior written permission, except in the case of brief quotations in critical reviews and certain other noncommercial uses permitted by copyright law.

Nebraska Writers Guild
PO Box 493
Scottsbluff, NE 69363

Cover Design by Kim Sosin

Verses from the Plains: A Poetry Collection

ISBN: 978-1-7357016-0-8 (paperback)
ISBN: 978-1-7357016-1-5 (ebook)

Library of Congress Control Number 2020919545

Contents

Foreword v

Green Leaves | *Susan Baron* 1
A Princess in Exile | *Zoe Baumel* 3
Alive and Berried/Ripe for the Picking | *D. S. Biggs* 6
Alive Here | *J. Eleanor Bonet* 9
Black Horse, Red Truck, Old Man | *j. kirk brown* 11
Death by Indifference | *j. kirk brown* 14
Easter in the Wood | *j. kirk brown* 15
Elderly Gardener | *j. kirk brown* 16
Before Renovation | *Lin Marshall Brummels* 17
Reported Missing | *Lin Marshall Brummels* 18
Encounter | *Marilyn June Coffey* 20
Mother's Needlework | *Marilyn Dorf* 21
Emergency Room Breakfast | *Marilyn Dorf* 22
The Reason for Darkness | *Marilyn Dorf* 24
What Poetry Is | *Marilyn Dorf* 25
Who Can Say | *Marilyn Dorf* 26
In the Absence of Memory | *Becky Faber* 27
I Was Her and She Was Me | *Grace Gugel* 29
State of the Union | *Neil Harrison* 31
In the Morning | *Bryant Holmes* 32
When Night Comes | *Jen Ippensen* 35
A Day at Auschwitz | *Sreekanth Kopuri* 36
Tomorrow | *Sreekanth Kopuri* 39
Death of George Floyd | *Karla Lester* 40
The Takeoff | *Scott L. Lucas* 42
Die-Cast Car | *James Luebbe* 43
Family Secret | *James Luebbe* 44
Mean Little Girl, Across Town | *James Luebbe* 45

Jackalope | *James Luebbe* 46
Parts Poem | *James Luebbe* 48
The Talk That Takes Us Far | *James Luebbe* 49
Losing the Body | *Clif Mason* 50
Four O Two | *Lillian McEvoy* 51
The Tree Talks Trash *(a poem for Arbor Day)* |
    Guadalupe J. Mier 52
Road Trip | *Ricardo Moran* 54
Herdin' Wild Pink Rabbits | *Charlene Neely* 56
Loss | *Julie S. Paschold* 59
Peas | *Julie S. Paschold* 61
How to Growl | *Holly Pelesky* 63
Priorities | *John Petelle* 65
Pastels in Grayscale | *John Petelle* 66
Natural Habitat | *Charlene Pierce* 68
Speed of the Valley | *Shyla Shehan* .70
Earth Hunger | *Rachel E. Smith* 72
Fuel | *Rachel E. Smith* 74
Howling at the Moon with My Mother | *Rachel E. Smith* . . .75
Inferno | *Rachel E. Smith* 76
Cost-Benefit Analysis: Spring 2020 | *Kim Sosin* 77
Minimum Maintenance Roads | *Kim Sosin* 78
Our River, Our Dance | *Kim Sosin* 80
The Cutting | *Nathan Sousek* 81
Setting | *Nathan Sousek* 82
Slow | *Nathan Sousek* 83

How to Find and Follow our Authors 85
Acknowledgments 87
Index by Author 89
Index by Title 91

Foreword

The best part of coordinating a poetry collection is having the ability to read all of the work fresh, to discover each one new, as if I'm standing in a garden and I'm able to sample every fruit, every vegetable, and every fresh new flower all to myself first. Thank you to the Nebraska Writers Guild for trusting me with such an honor and for creating a place for all of these voices to be heard.

In the following pages, you will find work from established poets and from new voices, all connected by the love of verse and the ability to put power behind their words. Some of the poems are sweet and sugary, and they will make you feel as warm as sunshine. Some are just for fun and will give you a good laugh to whet your appetite for more. Some are strong and will hit you hard but are needed for healing and validation. All provide needed nourishment. Allow yourself time to chew on each one and savor all it has to give.

Charlene Pierce
Project Coordinator

Green Leaves

Susan Baron

Green leaves dance outside the window. I lie in my crib and watch them. Backlit by sun, they move in shadowy patterns. My first memory.

Pouring salt onto the floor, round blue cardboard tucked under my arm because my hands are too small to hold it. Curious as it flows, making a white, conical pile. She finds it. Screams while she beats me. I am too young to know why pouring salt is wrong.

I am pleased to sit on my father's lap, leaning against his chest. The brightly lit room, mirrored in windows darkened by night. I am in pj's. Are they arguing? His arms wrapped around me. She can't hurt me.

I don't want to stop playing and come inside, so I wet my pants. I hide them because I should know better and am afraid of being shamed. She finds them, knows what they are and throws them in my face.

I am so sure I am not moving, but the hairbrush hits my head hard. "Stand still," she yells. The brush pulling and tearing, my head yanked back as she gathers the strands for braids. I leave for school with eyes full of tears.

He stops the attack by holding her arms, but she is able to reach around to his back and burn him with her cigarette. He doesn't hit her, only presses her to the wall, blocking her so she can't get at me. I turn and run from the house.

I am packing. This I will take. This I will leave. Clothes pile up. She leans in the doorway. "Are you leaving?" she asks. "You don't have to," she says. She doesn't say "I'm sorry."

Father sits holding my hand while we wait for my train to leave. His show of affection unusual, uncomfortable. There is something he wants to tell me. It comes out awkwardly. "Don't let your body be used," he says. "Don't get hurt." I almost laugh.

Green leaves dance outside the window. I begin new memories.

A Princess in Exile

Zoe Baumel

This care facility like an old-time,
main street, small town motel
individual bedrooms, desk, lamp and chair
All adult orphans, no family left
Most residents don't notice loneliness
It does not exist in their happiness
Minds filled with memories of long ago

Her royal family executed
Bloodied by the new regime
father, mother, groom
Grateful she escaped.
She understands her safety requires
confinement in this grand suite.
Stiff, grey, icy guards of the new regime,
with orders to arrest her if she leaves.

She looks out through beautiful
wall-length windows overlooking city life
hard urban smoothness, sleek skyscrapers,
stalagmites piercing foggy predawn quiet,
green and red and amber and white
blinking lights like lightning bugs

These pleasantries provide daily meaning:
Memories that engulf, endure
priceless antique furniture,

treasures delicate, finely oiled
Upright, prim, on her velvet chaise,
she enjoys this wonderful day, vivid memories,
clear and colorful, abundant life once lived,
and blissfully still lives

Fashions designed by the greatest names;
precious pendants, bracelets, baubles,
diamond, platinum, gold;
her magical wedding, perfection relished,
dancing, tender, loving intimacy cherished.

Startled she turns, the moment broken,
A helper enters with gleaming smile
"Who is this person? My hand maiden?"
white bonnet, white apron, black ballet shoes
The nurse aid in her flowered scrubs
to escort her for lunch. Her
far off voice whispers, coaxes.

She barely hears the words:
"It's time to leave this tiny room
with only one small window,
to join the others in the cafeteria"
filled with wheelchairs, canes,
and walkers all
attached to residents
like bionic appendages

The helper asks, smiling broadly,
"What did you dine on yesterday?"
She hears a voice, it
muffles through her jarred mind's fog.

Her furrowed brows intense, as
recent memories pop up jerkily
like old slides on a projector
Click-thunk, click-thunk, click-thunk
Black and white half visions of yesterday,
edges yellow and faded and cloudy with age

"Here at this facility we have a full menu."
The voice so smooth, so kind, alluring,
she accepts this invitation to dance.
Smiling as her ballroom gown,
silk and lace and sheer,
floats as she whirls and glides
to music only she can hear.
So grateful she escaped.

Alive and Berried/Ripe for the Picking

D. S. Biggs

Part 1:
It was the berry picking,
her hands a little blue
like her thinning hair.
But her knees were good,
her eyes were clear
and her laughter was
the song of a tougher generation.
Of a people wiser in their senility
than those who never stop
chasing tomorrow's dreads
long enough to savor
the warm earth before
being swallowed by it.

Oh yes, it was always the berry picking.
And maybe a little of her stubbornness.
Of being able to wring
the neck of a chicken,
or make a quilt,
or bury a husband
and several offspring
and never fear
months without rain
or that the pantry
would ever be empty.
To visit a cemetary

every Sunday
and kneel beside a grave
and hear his voice,
"There must be berries again this year,
your hands are a little blue."
To smile at his whimsy,
leak a little juice from somewhere
resembling her tearducts,
tidy the plot
and make her way slowly
to her hybrid minivan
and then, even more slowly,
to the exit—
Alive and in the moment,
without so much as a passing thought
as to when the Angel of Death
might get his fingers a little blue
from picking *her*.

Part 2:
The Angel of Death
has his fingers in many pies,
but not the ones on her windowsill.
These are special pies,
reserved for family and friends—
though they may not
see her again, or she them.
The pies are constants,
like butterflies and rainbows,
to ward off what might pass
for sadness, if she stopped long enough
for sorrow to make her bluer
than her berries.

True, she's barely known it to happen,
but sometimes crows
do ignore the straw man
in her late husband's overalls.

Part 3:
Prologue:
"She had the heart of a lion."
"And the stomach of one, too!"
[Laughter]
"Oh yes, she enjoyed a good meal—
was a damn fine cook."
"Mostly, yeah, but those pies!
Lordy, she couldn't make crust
for love nor money!"

Epilogue:
If there's a story worth telling, tell it.
If a thing is worth remembering,
remember it.
If tomorrow is a dream,
today's the beginning of
its fulfilment.

Part 4:
Should *anything* have four parts?
Ask a barbershop quartet.

Alive Here

J. Eleanor Bonet

No one lives here anymore.
I visit often, my sole companion is myself.
The broken farmhouse offers shelter still.
Flip-flop-softened footsteps wake the crooked tread.
Weathered raw by sun and rain, its rusty nails
No longer grip the wood.

Despite its blistered paint and desiccated rope,
The porch and swing invite this restless woman's weight,
Heavy though the years have made me, I trust its strength.
It creaks as if to greet me as it did the child, the girl and lover.
My tiptoes push to start a syncopated sway
To hypnotize and harmonize the memories it will stir.

Drifting into conscious dreams, I float within my recollected life.
It enfolds and cradles me, enthralling me in memories from a
    distance.
Emotions cleared of pain, allow a soulful sojourn in childhood's
    delights.
Love is stored in all the senses. No anger. No sorrow. No guilt.
Laughter is as joyous in the mind as when released in youth.
Moments in the now unfurl, becoming hours, days, and years of
    living then.

Cooling sweat wanders through my scalp, escapes behind my ear,
To run along my neck, reminding me
Of timeless mother-daughter moments.

My skin relives the feel of gentle, roughened fingers
Lifting dampened tresses, Ma blowing the heat away.
I giggled then; I smile now.

Shadows move within the fading light, revealing time exists,
But at a different pace when then returns to now.
Oppressive stillness draws a curtain down, shutting out the dream.
I push my toe against the floor, wanting to restart the pendulum,
To move the air through force of rhythmic pitch and sway,
Willing time and weather bend to my desire.

A wayward cooling draft builds frigid gusts,
Pushed by powers beyond my will,
The house responds. It breathes. I moan. The wind howls.
The porch's centenary wood reacts in noisy chorus with
    cicadas' song.
Bees and beetles buzz. Sounds merge. Silence descends.
They are heralds of a coming storm.

I feel a pulse within me, change is rolling in on thunder.
The barometric force rebounds and urges action.
Sulfur moths take flight across the sea of tender grains.
Those wingbeats call the tempest down to thump the dust.
The earth revives, her thirst is quenched, and we sigh.
I find myself entirely alive here, waiting for the storm to pass.

Black Horse, Red Truck, Old Man

j. kirk brown

He seemed an old man to me, then
The weathered and wiry cowboy
Rolling a cigarette as he leaned on the fender
Of a faded red pickup truck
That had slid off the logging road
And come to a precarious rest
On the mountainside
Two tires ripped from their rims

"Are you OK?"
The 1960s version of me hollered down to him
Clad in my chambray shirt, bell bottom jeans and desert boots

"I'm fine." He hollered back to the me who was
A week away from classes beginning again
At a university 800 miles to the east
And 8,000 feet below where I was that day

"You need a ride? I haven't seen another vehicle
up here all day."

"Could you take me down to Dubois?
I gotta try and make a phone call."

"Sure. C'mon. Get in."

He was the same wrangler
I had spoken with two days before

While I was hiking
Up the valley from where I was camped

He was sitting up on a squat, black horse
The reins loose in hands so leathery
I thought, at first, he was wearing gloves
He thanked me for not spooking the group of cows
I had inadvertently hiked into

He never got down
But we talked for a while about nothing much

He was living alone in a line shack
"Up the mountain a bit. Just me and Jack here."
He was looking for a bull he needed to vaccinate
But he couldn't find him

He talked about his boy, "About your age, I'd guess."
"I didn't raise him much, but I hear he's a good kid."
He said with some pride
"He got drafted and now he's a door gunner on a helicopter in
    Viet Nam."
He shook his head
"I'm not even sure where that is, exactly."

As he rode away, he looked back over his shoulder
"I ain't talked with nobody for must be at least three weeks."
Then he said, "Thanks."
Like I'd given him a gift

It wasn't quite ten in the morning
But a cloud of alcohol got into the car with him
"Jack never run me off the road like that
and I've been drunk on him hundreds of times."

"What's taking you into town, Bud?"

He turned his wet, drunken eyes toward me
"Word just got up to me late yesterday.
My boy's dead.
I'm just hoping the number I have for his mother is still good.
I think I may have missed the funeral."

Death by Indifference

j. kirk brown

I am a diabetic
I have hypertension
I am over 70 years of age
COVID-19 snacks
Upon people like me

Yet I see my fellow humans
Becoming bored with caution
Becoming bored with caring

They want to shop
They want to gather
They want to play, again

I understand

My death
And the deaths of others like me
Have become a small price to pay
To party

Easter in the Wood

j. kirk brown

While those blessed with faith
Gather among the lilies and the incense
In hopeful anticipation of their next life

I lie here resting in the wood
Dappled in birdsong
and morning light

And behold

Up through the tattered twill of my shirt
Up through the bony cage within which my heart once beat
And my lungs once gave breath to song
Rises a wild flower
Which has drawn upon my essence in the earth
To bloom

And in that flower
I am risen

Elderly Gardener

j. kirk brown

I work the ground alone now
Unaccompanied and unencumbered
By the desires of others

I bury myself
in the work

I bury myself
with the roots of every tree, shrub and flower

I dig little graves
and place life into them

My sweat soaks the soil

There is an urgency about the planting
I have never experienced before

I no longer take for granted
the next spring
the next summer
the next fall

Before Renovation

Lin Marshall Brummels

Walking about the empty showroom's
stacks and piles of debris left behind
when Shopko closed its doors
is like exploring an abandoned house
where a family fled in the night
with only the clothes on their backs.

The day before renovation is slated
to transform the mess, we find pencils,
coat hangers, cards, and leftover toys
amongst the trash, men's briefs
tucked behind the service counter.

There's a second floor, unnoticed
by customers when business thrived,
full of offices and conference rooms
with kitchens attached, big enough
to house five homeless families.

Discarded computers, cash registers,
optical equipment, built-in cabinets,
and desks litter the offices, while
hundreds of cage-like storage units
stand empty, as if someone opened doors
at a zoo and let the animals escape.

Reported Missing
Lin Marshall Brummels

Arthropoda, Lepidoptera and Hymenoptera
reported missing on the evening news
    Asian beetles gone from soy fields
    crickets vanished from garages
    Monarchs decline without milkweeds

Honeybees declared essential
    for pollinating crops and gardens,
    most susceptible to chemical drift
        endangered

Commissioners worry it's an outside job,
    appoint squad to search for kidnappers
    fret about foreign agents
    wait for ransom notes

Detectives assigned to investigate,
dig into task like Sherlock Holmes disciples
    find spiders in flower beds,
    boxelder bugs in barns and wood piles,
        hiding like nuclear fallout survivors

Prosecutors pursue usual suspects,
    find only winged carpenter ant queens
    dressed for Halloween
        casing houses to infest

Commentators speculate about state
    of nature and agriculture
    worry about future food supply,
        starving people

Legislators terrified of losing big money gifts
    bow to Bayer, Monsanto, Syngenta,
    fail to act
        again

Encounter

Marilyn June Coffey

The huge, pale green luna moth
materializes out of the June night
to flutter persistently against my window screen.

Mesmerized by my forty watt bulb,
again and again it flings its fuzzy body,
fat as my finger,
against the metal barrier, then clings:
its huge wings forming green fans
its long tails ending in droplets.

I stare,
bow reverently before the chance
that brings the luna moth here
in this instant of mortal time.
Then I turn off the light.
set us both free

Mother's Needlework

Marilyn Dorf

My mother, always stitching, always sewing,
whether in the farmhouse or her garden where she

aligned her seeds like hooks and eyes down grooves
of dirt precisely cut as the fragile tissue patterns

she so artfully laid out and followed, aiming her needle
arrow-like and accurate, whipping like a bird beak up and down,

her fabrics blooming bright as pansies and nasturtiums,
each nested in its buttonhole of sod. My mother,

always humming, and her trusty Singer singing,
creating dresses, skirts and blouses, mending, too,

and patching father's shirts and overalls, their seams
ripped all asunder by his hoisting everything

from bales of hay to baby calves. And my mother
keeping pace, always stitching, always sewing.

Emergency Room Breakfast

Marilyn Dorf

Quick breakfast
from Bosselman's
eaten in a wheelchair

outside the emergency
room door
so I won't pass out

waiting for the doctor
to examine you,
waiting for the dim

scratch of his voice
to become bold
and make sense

while watching a young
intern nodding off
at his desk,

someone's heartbeats
thumping across
a monitor

and one cockroach
scuttling
past,

rattled as
a young nurse
late for work.

The Reason for Darkness

Marilyn Dorf

Hair uncombed, she stood
at the cusp of evening,
waiting for darkness to
wrap like a robe about her
slim self, the silk of it sleek
on her arms, as she watched
it clothe the trees, the hills
and valleys, silence slipping
through its fingers slick as
the voles and the leaf-bugs;
the moon on hiatus, stars
peeping out one by one.
And there, wrapped close
in that garment of darkness,
she rode out the night, until
the stars closed their eyelids
at dawn. It is then that she
went back home, knowing.
Knowing at last the reason
for darkness, for ravens
and grackles, the grinding
and growling of thunder.

What Poetry Is

Marilyn Dorf

it is the red-crested cardinal, unaware of the pandemic,
calling you out to sing and to dance and to rejoice.

it is a squirrel, furred and coiffed to the fullest,
scurrying, scheming, not knowing what's next

it is a woodrat gnawing the floorboard
under your kitchen, wanting to be written down

it is a camel, ideas galore, some unsolved and
unwritten, all bundled dutifully onto her back

it is a mosquito, buzzing and bothering, itching for
a taste of the ideas sitting on hold just under your skin

it is a zebra, dressed up in pure black and white,
every stripe faithful to rhythm and rhyme

it is a woodpecker rat-a-tat-tatting the tree bark,
searching for that one last lost word

it is a screech owl haunting and harassing
the dark of your soul

it is the full moon, bloated bleed-red and bursting,
trying to contain its outburst of laughter

Who Can Say

Marilyn Dorf

Who can say
that stars
are not poems
unpublished,
defenseless,
their luster,
their lyrics,
sprinkling
over the ease
of the night?

Who can say
that the owls
do not take them
to heart, hook
them onto their
clipboards to
take home and
read during
the dark of
their day?

In the Absence of Memory

Becky Faber

In the absence of memory
there is only today,
a crossword puzzle with no clues

black and white events
of a simple life
(if there is such a thing)
twisted into a complex
grey,
each occasion
a fragment of all previous ones

She forgets the recent,
the obvious,
the fact that she forgets

What she cannot forget:
her grudges,
mostly against her siblings,
their old bones on display
in nursing homes,
eyes blinded by life,
legs weakened by this
journey
to the age
where we all hope
to be comforted

by our
common
memories

I Was Her and She Was Me

Grace Gugel

Woman is a coffee table
Her legs are thin and quaint
She is most enjoyed with an arched back
She never takes up too much space
She is allowed few imperfections
Her skin holds water rings—Woman is expected to endure many
(No rings and she's a prude
More than one ring and she's skanky)
Decorators *always* rather have swanky

Woman is a chandelier
Whose bulbs must simultaneously light and dim themselves
She must be freshly polished
She must complement the room—But never be the center of
    attention
She is best enjoyed when she blends into her surroundings

Woman is a scented candle
Her smell must be nothing but pleasant—hint of lavender,
    maybe honey
She glitters and lights up a room with her cooperative burning
As a lady, she must never let her wick wilt or grey
She never shows her wax spitting or dripping
She is expected to make the home and warm her guests
But flickering and licking with her flames is punished

Woman is a sentimental knickknack
She must pose while on display
She must blow the dust from her own shoulders
It is imperative that she holds her fragile self together—real
    women never show cracks
And when she knows that something better is coming
She must tuck herself away behind the brittle bound books

State of the Union

Neil Harrison

This hanging rug
depicts a desert scene—
black clouds shrouding
a golden sun
beyond scattered saguaros
and a lone horse
pawing at a dry
creek bed, seeking
the buried source of life.

Against the wall
coarse burlap anchors
the colored tufts of yarn,
secure backing for this
stark symbol
of obstinate faith—
because we must
we will soon find
water in this desert.

In the Morning

Bryant Holmes

In the morning,
This morning,
In the wake of the storm,
Snowfall buried the dead.
It fell upon the tanks
That had given up their ghosts.
It fell in the trenches,
In the mire and the mud,
On artillery unused,
On pins unpulled,
On sidearms forever holstered.
It fell upon the bloodied and dirtied face of the soldier,
Into his wide and unblinking eyes,
Onto his face, streaked like a crying child's.
It fell upon the allies and their enemies,
Upon the victor and the vanquished,
Upon the colorless faces of those
Whose names would soon be swallowed by history,
This morning.

In the morning,
This morning,
Under the eye of the rising sun,
The house awoke with a start,
With the sudden smack! of newspaper
Against the door.
The children awoke soon after,

Laughing and carrying on as children do,
As only children can.
They marched downstairs with their blankets,
In their bedclothes, and warmed themselves before
The television, the only friend awaiting them this early.
"We mustn't wake Mother!" warned the oldest,
Thinking of her mother,
Upstairs in her dark room
At the end of a darker hallway.
"And what of Father?" asked the youngest,
Who looked like the father they all missed.
"Father," said the oldest. "We shall have to pray for Father."
It was too late for Mother,
For she was already awake,
Ejected from her delicate slumber,
But anchored to her side of the bed,
Her eyes red and swollen,
Her face streaked with tears like her once-blinking husband's.

Later in the morning,
This morning,
Downstairs at the breakfast table,
The children played with their food,
And the news on the television,
And the newspaper on the table beside Mother's cup,
Spoke solemnly
Of the war that Father was in.
And what the newspaper didn't say,
Because Mother fervently prayed for it not to,
And what the children didn't know,
Because Mother fervently prayed for them not to,
And what Mother knew but didn't want to know or admit,
Was that Father was buried in the snow,

The snow that fell upon his bloody and bruised face,
And into his unblinking eyes,
And turned him as immobile as marble,
The snow that would soon leave only
His vague outline as a monument
That neither his children nor wife would ever visit.

The same snow that fell
And buried the fallen,
Earlier in the morning,
This morning.

When Night Comes

Jen Ippensen

She lies on her side, curled into a fetal position, as always, craving warmth and comfort, yearning for protection. Like so many others, she has a bad back. Too many years of stupid mistakes. Too long carrying herself and others—Matriarch by default, thanks to cancer—paying rent and later the mortgage, twins in car seats dangling one from each arm and her a tipping scale, working to pay off college loans, car loans, credit card bills. Struggling to fill the gas tank with long hours, bloody tongue.

They say she should sleep on her back. She tries. Unfolds herself to vulnerability. Face up in the dark. Thinks this is what it feels like to lie in a coffin. Imagines a rose, or carnation—they're cheaper—clasped in waxy hands folded over her midsection. Imagines crumbling away to nothing. Focuses on air entering and leaving her body. Convinces herself it means something. Convinces herself she's too young to die, to find something to live for until morning. Maybe a child's smile, a cup of coffee, a pen in her hand. She curls onto her side, arms wrapped around her eventual corpse.

A Day at Auschwitz

Sreekanth Kopuri

(after visiting the Auschwitz concentration camp, Poland)

A bleak sunless morning
would be right to know the

meaning of death and meaning's
own. The wheels of Krakow bus

are burdened with our curiosity,
stagger and screech to halt at the

"Museum Auschwitz" stop
at last. The ash flakes of

my long soaked dream spill
down on the rusty gates of

The Shame open for the
visitors today, showcasing

the tatters of six million silences
disgorging streams of visitors

like the omens coming alive
from the skulled memories of

the dead innocents' lost dreams.
This is what we are dressed in

our Sunday best for, on a picnic-
spree, making a line of humans

to know the synonyms of a naked
truth of those cattle-lines, saunter

through the arched promise –
arbeit macht frei, on a terminal

earth's long crumpled scroll of
roll calls into a silence occasionally

broken by the invisible chirrups
from the sentient chestnut trees along

into the cold sooty furnaces gaped
open with the weight of a million

absences, displaying *Men in
Striped Pyjamas* who live hanged

in portraits on blackened white-
washed walls of the Aryan pride

engraved *a race that must be totally
exterminated* –Hans Frank 1944.

My cam trespasses to steal the preserved
vengeance in those blinded spectacles,

shaving brushes, prayer mats, shoes,
children's clothes, dolls and seven

thousand dark coiled remains of its fury
—the fleeces, showcased in the frozen

eyeballs of history, only a fraction of
a hatred's weight. A fourth generation

visitor breaks down at the sight of the
preserved hair when an usher reminds us

silence. My footprints sign a testimony
on the ashes of this graveyard of leftovers

of an apocalyptic trial—a failed
succession of a delusive visionary.

Tomorrow

Sreekanth Kopuri

After the nuclear winter, when
the waters turn into its soot

a lost child walks alone shouldering
burnt violins to perform the earth's last rites

a lonely scorpion searches
for the bleeding love that can melt the stones,

it will be time the long secrets
will hold mirror to your heart and

the truth will break its silence among
the cries that will be the only grains of sand

so if you have a day to undo
the legacy of that primordial void

it will be perhaps when a lion
weans a lamb or an eagle a dove.

As the clock is still green
let the hands wreathe a rainbow

around this earth
to warn against our arms.

Death of George Floyd

Karla Lester

There is no justice for George Floyd
George Floyd's neck and God-made cheek pinned to the street
    like a roped steer
Breathing in tire rubber for his last breath
he was only asking to keep breathing in the tire rubber
pinned down to the man-poured street
I can't breathe
Separate out the injustices
Call out each of the crimes:
first the profiling,
then the targeting,
then the baiting,
then the igniting,
gasoline on the flame,
then the bargaining,
then the takedown,
the pinning on the ground (knee to neck),
more bargaining,
then the decision to stay on the neck,
I can't breathe
Then every measure of time multiplied by God's infinite
    universe to ignore his pleas, not even pleas, just him
    saying,
I can't breathe
George Floyd was murdered on the streets of his city in broad
    daylight,

For being a child of God
Created by and with the infinite power and beauty and
    goodness of all of the universe
George Floyd was created
In God's likeness
by the hand of God

The Takeoff

Scott L. Lucas

Buckled into the aircraft seat as it begins to taxi.
The seat belts will help (if we hit a car or something).
Most crashes happen in takeoff.
I check my dental work with my tongue.
It's all there, distinctive as a fingerprint.
If they find my head they'll know it's me.
Dr. Mike will say, "That's him alright."
"I would know those bridges and deciduous teeth anywhere,
though he hasn't been flossing."
This time I didn't make it past the do-it-yourself insurance booth.
I bet $7 against their $100,000 that they'd get me killed this time.
As they power up
I smile and nod reassuringly to the nervous lady beside me.
Then I lean back,
look straight ahead,
grip my armrests firmly with my hands,
and my seat firmly with my butt cheeks,
as I await sudden death over Omaha.

Die-Cast Car

James Luebbe

Ellie, digging in her sandpile,
strikes metal, that first abrupt chink
clean as the closing of a lid.
She sets to work, blood abeat
with the news of something lost,
and quickly brings it up –
a yellow die-cast car,
faded to the last pale petals
of autumn goldenrod.
She brings it to me,
cheeks flushed, eyes alive
with questions. "Whose is it?
How did it get there?"
"A boy who lived here
before you," I say,
forcing the words out even,
but feeling them back up
in a low reluctant mound.

Family Secret

James Luebbe

It is a simple oval pebble,
just small enough to hold
unseen and pass between
ourselves discretely.
It is so odd-shaped, when
we bring it out again
to see, we are sure to find it
strangely curved, freshly flawed,
a crack appears anew.
We pass it around once more
showing ourselves how
the sun reflects it
differently each day, how
the crystalled glaze has weathered
like a face, and how its heft
gets lighter with the years,
yet larger, harder to conceal,
demanding its release.

Mean Little Girl, Across Town

James Luebbe

York, Nebraska, 1928

Every afternoon we ran
the downhill block past
the Methodist Church,
then turned our separate ways
for home. Next block
had a snarling fenced black dog.
I knew it had waited
for me all day long.
"I'm not going home alone,"
I yelled. "Not today."
I yanked at their hair, dragged them,
fought like a little fury
to keep them with me.
A car drove by.
The driver saw those five mean girls
fighting with his child. Next year,
father moved us near a new school.
I never told him it was my fight.

Jackalope
James Luebbe

The last surviving Jackalope
in Keith County, Nebraska
sits on a shelf in
Ole's Big Game Lounge
trying not to flinch when
drinkers chink their Hamm's
beneath his nose
hurrahing the local boys
who have won again.
Whiskers twitching,
Patsy Cline playing
on the Sebring Select-O-Matic
and his eyes level at me
to keep it all between us.
The skinny thing looks starved
above inch and a half thick
t-bone steaks, one eye wandering
to the rigid coyote,
weight shifting toward haunches
in case the wolverine
or bobcat moves.
He'll sneak back
to the kitchen after closing
grabbing nibbles on a carrot
or lettuce greens, enough
to get him by,
embodying all the best

of the Platte River Valley
that ever was,
or ever should have been.

Parts Poem

James Luebbe

Roy Cast says we come
from practical stock
and don't buy new until
a thing is all used up,
stretched out, made to do
a little longer. This one's
been growing weeds
for three decades now,
a silver maple pushing
between the trunk and bumper,
sparrow splatters coloring
outside the lines
of its cracked windshield.
It was built around a big block
limerick, stroked and bored
with a two-barrel Holley couplet.
The starter is gone,
sold off to a sonnet
that neatly fit.
The radio eats my eight track tapes,
its loose antenna strobing elegies
or strangling odes.
Hey Roy, want to get that
old clunker of yours running?
I've got a tight four-speed metaphor
that's yours if you need it,
or a couple interesting rhymes
with plenty of tread.

The Talk That Takes Us Far

James Luebbe

There appeared the singularity of a word
In someone's mind and it may have hung there
For years waiting for the fire to light,
Waiting to explode mind to mind
In sounds and images,
From lips to lips in joys, desires and visions
That no one had known they possessed.
Then the long conversations began, before birth,
In the womb, the falling stars of mothers' sighs,
Trailing the sparks of their wishes,
A shower of bright meteors raining inward
From fathers, sisters, grandparents,
Starting that first internal talk in our heads
That lasts a lifetime, that spins its galaxy within us,
That informs each taste, each sound, each kiss.
It puts a word to "sweet," to "chime," to "love,"
That long singular human talk
That takes us far,
Then walks us all back home.

Losing the Body

Clif Mason

He was losing his fingerprints, as children lost baby teeth, as adults lost dreams. With its black pruning hook, autumn night lopped the heads of summer's last roses. Leaves dropped like golden rain & the grass began its long dreamless sleep.

What good did it do him to deny his loss? Did it make him any more whole? Could he also get along without ear lobes or eyebrows? Toenails or the riverine veins in his forearms?

Moonbeams' goblets shattered on the street & a screech owl called from a red oak tree. The owl's talons owned a clarity autumn air could not equal.

People who still had fingerprints no doubt had faith they truly distinguished them from every other of the planet's billions. He wished instead to be indistinguishable, anonymous as dust motes spinning in a bright beam of light.

Leaves spiraled to the street & the owl's cold eyes scanned the ground. He was grateful one of the men he might have been was not the man he'd become.

Four O Two

Lillian McEvoy

4:02 PM – London
10:02 AM – Omaha
caught somewhere between
the fable of time
the inaccuracy of my watch
and the capacity of my bladder
caught between the top of clouds and the bottom of stars
the air is negative 61.6 degrees Fahrenheit—
I still haven't perfected the British speech yet.
Suspended like trapped angels
no leg room, filled overhead compartment
watch screens on the backs of heads
we are all headed to the same place to depart in such separate
    ways
miles and miles from home, no metric system
complimentary ice cream
disposable ginger ale readily spillable
"seatbelts on" dings and is consistently ignored
time is a myth and so is God.

The Tree Talks Trash *(a poem for Arbor Day)*

Guadalupe J. Mier

Do not Daylight Saving Time me,
    says the tree;
'tis I that depend on the seasons.
Ye shall not steal my hours;
do not claim my time.

The motion of the planet
and the tug of its moon
affect me more
than your clicking
the big hands back 60 ticks,
    or whatever
    you
    digitally do
    now:
digitally, digitally, duh!?

I do not tickity-tock — no ears to hear.
See the sun? It wears no cartoon shades
to lessen the light.
So don't think that the hands of a clock
can determine the length of my shadows.

I have my cycle; it's a natural rule,
a law of Mother Nature.
My leaves may shudder and shake
come the eclipse,

but they will unfurl to taste the light
at the rebirth of the sun;
nuff said.
I must shake the squirrels
away that are playing with my nuts;
time to go . . .

Road Trip

Ricardo Moran

I heard an old Chevy
near Alliance
humming a new tune.

Between the rivers
of Platte and Wood, the sandhill
cranes folded light into grey.

While in the back seat
Valentine strung a Broken Bow,
hitchhiking a love song
to Grand Island.

Just then, my Alma rolled past me
in a Buick no less,
laughing into the future
while our car buzzed
like a dragonfly to Riverton.

There, I sat on the sidewalk
waiting for the children to visit
the corner market, where a tree
now grows through the cash register.

Later that afternoon,
while in a Funk, I admired
the Red Clouds over Blue Hill

and listened to a melody floating
in from Bladen.

With cassette tapes whirling tunes,
I swung by Hebron to pick up a Friend
and we met Beatrice in Steele City
who recited Kooser's poetry
all the way to Brownville,
to see Rudloff smile one more time.

But it was Lincoln, and then Omaha that pulled me
Northward. When I kneeled
before St. Cecilia, someone who looked
like me trembled in the pew ahead.

Outside, Mason led his flock of bombers,
while in Bancroft, Neihardt wove dreams into stories.
And my friend Gandy sang from afar.

The Chevy and I said our goodbyes.
And I hiked along the waters of the Elkhorn,
to find the spirit of the Cowboy,
to find a new way home.

Herdin' Wild Pink Rabbits

Charlene Neely

This was way back in the early 60s
when things were a lot rougher in the Hay Market
back in those days of flower power and free love,
they thought nothing of turning loose
a couple hundred pink rabbits every hour or two
up on the 3rd floor of the old candy factory

as soon as those critters were released from their molds
wild strawberry rabbits as big as my hand,
they tumbled and spilled and walked on their ears
in their dash for what they thought was freedom.
As soon as they squeezed through the hole in the wall
they were trapped on a conveyor belt 8 feet above the
                                          floor.

It dashed their still soft bodies into gooey pile-ups
as it made a sharp right and then another
onto a wider path that drew them downward
somersaulting and hand-standing—
or should I say ear-standing—
to a six foot wide belt below.

Here's where I entered the story.
That wide belt was fitted with a wire rack
that shuffled back and forth
meant to corral the smaller, firmer

jelly strips and shuttle them into neat rows
as they entered the Dark Chocolate Waterfall.

My job was to corral those rabbits,
stretch them out neatly on trays that continuously
wandered in a zig-zag pattern
toward that forbidden waterfall,
for Pink Rabbits were meant
for Milk Chocolate coats only.

So amid the crashing and falling rabbits
at each corner and the drifting trays
filled with finally subdued rabbits whose
katywampus, cock-eyed ears were settling
into rigor mortis when they should be laid out
all straight and erect.

Too big to stuff in my mouth,
too wriggly to tuck in my shirt.
I couldn't save them from falling
or being turned to mush. All else failing,
I laughed, remembering the *I Love Lucy* bit
where Lucy and Ethel worked in a candy factory.

I gradually coaxed and corralled
the majority of the critters,
hearded them down sticky floored halls
to be bathed in Milk Chocolate ponds
and perched in the fake grass
of some child's Easter Basket.

So, if some late night wandering
the streets of the Hay Market

you think you see, out of the corner
of your eye, a Pink Rabbit hopping
from one side of the street to the other
you may be right—

    Watch out! There may be more!

Loss

Julie S. Paschold

I'm walking my usual route
from car to office
down the main street sidewalk of this small town
burdened with bags and thoughts
about to greet the pair of chickadees
who live atop the building
on the way
when I almost step on
a bright yellow spot
left on the concrete.
It is an egg, fallen
from my friends' nest
during yesterday's storm.
I greet them with a sad smile,
careful to step over
what could have been their progeny.
Later, proceeding through my own grief
and enraged at one person's ability
to willingly deceive and parasitize
I wonder at the small songbirds' loss
and if they also felt wronged or sorrow.

Dear chickadees, do you grieve?
Did you fly down in angst
and wish the deed undone,
the pain unfelt?
Were you outraged at the wind for being wronged?

And if you did, little ones,
what song did you chirp,
what sunrise did you beckon to,
what sky did you fly towards
to ease your burden?
Oh, please, dear friends
can you share with me
the melody
to sing away this pain?

Peas

Julie S. Paschold

I had taken the peas from the freezer
the day before.
They are now in an old pickle jar
and I on the edge of a small city pond.
Two sets of Canada goslings and their parents reside near me
one with an orange beaked grey
sort of uncle honking his directions
to all of us, keeping even the lone goose standing
beside me
in line.
Shaking a small fistful into my hand, I swing
up
and let the legumes fly
the small green spheres
plopping
pop pop pop   pop   pop
onto the water in a pleasing announcement
and goose butts rise,
beaks scoop and dip
the uncle honks
we in our respective hemispheres
gently bumping each other
rubbing pleasant mornings together
sharing this air,
this Sunday morning,
these peas
peas and please and thank you

pop pop pop   plop   pop
honk
as even a robin tilts his head toward me
in greeting
or breakfast
looking for that unsuspecting worm.

We here sharing peace
and space
for these few moments
here
on this earth we are all borrowing
from our children.

How to Growl

Holly Pelesky

Honey, when you wake
in the middle of the night, see your mama
awake still, staring out the window,
I know you can't see this wolf I once tried to keep
off my back, you only know it looks like sadness.

Those mornings crying in bed, it was her howl
trapped in my throat. Afternoons on the treadmill,
that was your mama trying to outrun her, knowing
she had sniffed me out again, that she would be
here soon, curling me into bed, whimpering.

Once I thought I was gaining distance
from her hungry jaws wanting to consume
my flesh in giant mouthfuls. But when
I turned to look at her, I saw I wasn't afraid
anymore. I had fallen in love
with her paws padding after me,
that pant for my presence.

You see, it's lucky to be loved, even when
all that's loving you is your own sadness.

Now my fingernails grow fast and long.
My hair has matted. I wonder
where my tame has gone.
She can't sink her teeth into me now

I've grown fangs of my own.
When I turn my head, no one
is behind me, it's just my own legs
running, running, running.

Go to bed, baby. Sleep. Dream of something
happy. In the morning we'll read your books
from the library and I'll tell you which
animals make the best mothers.

Priorities

John Petelle

Jasmine spent her last forty-three dollars
on oil paints instead of food.
After four days of fasting,
her brush pulled colors
from veins to canvas.

She put seven paintings on the walls
of her ghetto's coffee shop.

A grey-haired man in an Armani suit
bought the whole series.

Jasmine sank to her knees
and wept
in the corner aisle of Aldi's
having traded her children
for macaroni.

Pastels in Grayscale

John Petelle

I want to think about something beautiful.
Raw and glorious,
stealing my breath.
Like a starving child
clawing the last piece of bread from a street vendor's cart.

> But dark thoughts find me,
> unsavory bill collectors of my bitter past.
> Cold riptide sweeps my legs.
> I choke on salt, among the sharks.

I want to think about the splendid majesty.
Low-hanging clouds,
a luminous wreath on sun-kissed hills.
My hermit friend enshrines them just so;
I bend my mind's vision toward the peaks.

> The sharks return. Circling.
> Dead black eyes in all directions.
> Jagged razors engulf me,
> I see the red mist billow, my liquid coffin fills.

I want to think about the delicacy
of my daughter's smile.
Skipping in the front yard,
nine years old, by the yellow lawn sprinkler,
brown pigtails dancing.

                          White teeth flash,
                   the sphere of desolate eyes
                          collapses onto me.
                I am dismembered from every side.

And all I want,
is to think about the lovely scenes,
the treasured memories,
which flee from my desperation,

                    as I falter, and drop memory's key.

Natural Habitat

Charlene Pierce

Wind cuts through
tight skyscrapers
snakes after prey swallowing
blown hats and lost umbrellas
like hors d'oeuvres.

People scramble
fight over taxis, rush
home before the sky pushes
down the sun.

Before the storm
before the hail
before the lightning
before the sirens
sound
before they get stuck
between work and home,
stuck in the gullet
of the city.

Stuck with strangers, packed
shoulder to shoulder, toe to toe
in the back storage room,
staring at the purchases in their hands
trying to remember why
they needed it now.

Somewhere,
far from here,
people are tucked in
their homes, doors locked,
windows closed, curtains drawn
into each other.

Lights shut out before they recede
each to their own
bed where they lie
staring at the ceiling, wishing
it was open to the sky.

Speed of the Valley

Shyla Shehan

Silicon Valley just doesn't understand—
they don't even speak the same language.
Caffeinated traffic moves so fast
every flat plastic scrap molded
with the imprint of 16 digits
gets used up quicker than the last.
Tossed out like yesterday's takeout—
cut and pasted until nothing is left
of the original. Right-sized
and minimized into a system tray,
archived to an external hard drive,
never to be seen again—a landfill destiny
in a disposable world. The sinewy rise and fall
of each hot commodity forgotten
faster than the last. Slow down

the earthly turn
and watch the rise
and fall
of your lover's chest
at 2 a.m.
The rise
and fall of the night—
your daughter
and her first date. The color
of her dress and smile
and blush.

Some boy
will break her heart
or she'll break his.
I've missed
too much
already.

Earth Hunger

Rachel E. Smith

She mixes up a batch of homemade bread.
Grain and yeast of earth meet in sky blue bowl,
are warmed by water.

She stirs and dough sheets from the spoon
in velvety skeins, stretching
then breaking.

She scrapes the earth baby
from its sky blue womb,
lays it on the counter on a bed of flour.

She uses her hands (no bread machine for her),
pats flour all around, pushes, folds, turns
and pushes again until the earth baby glistens.

She calls to her youngest grandchildren.
They pull kitchen chairs to the counter,
kneel at the altar of earth and sky.

They poke and prod, tentative, and
then chubby hands burrow deep
into the warm, yeast-blessed mound.

They push, fold, turn, and push
again, following her movements,
brows furrowed, hands greedy,

voracious, feeding a hunger
they didn't know
they had.

Fuel

Rachel E. Smith

I fall asleep and dream of a one room schoolhouse
filled with nothing but books on shelves spiraled
round and round. The pages are crisp and clean,
old and tattered. They smell like vanilla.
I pull books from the shelves, pile
them into a ladder, reading as I go.
I find old friends, make new acquaintances,
read of killers and kings, butchers and bankers.
I fight wars and build cities, tear them down again,
learn art and poetry, fly a spaceship to Mars.
I become a pirate in the Caribbean,
race camels in Morocco, milk goats in the Himalayas.
I fill myself with words, light myself with knowledge.
It shoots from my fingertips like sparks,
sets the walls on fire. They blaze hot and bright
as I burn myself awake.

Howling at the Moon with My Mother

Rachel E. Smith

"Come howl at the moon," I say, and my mother
leaves blankets, warmed by cherry-pit packs,
just for me. Everyone should have such a mother.
We stand on the porch, seduced
by the scent of lilacs, snap pictures
and howl at the orb, hanging
over our heads, gravid with possibility.

A moon as pregnant as the mare
just before she gave birth
to the foal sheltered at her flank,
legs splayed, ears swiveled toward our howls
in light that paints his white spots with silver.

Inferno

Rachel E. Smith

Tongues of autumn race along branches,
crisp leaves to scarlet, topaz, gamboge.
Aureolin fingers stroke trees, ignite saffron trails
detonate mahogany, umber, vermillion.

Crimson explosions burn, blister leaves
with russet hunger, light magenta pyrotechnics,
consume every leaf on every tree.

An inferno of goldenrod, ochre, sienna
bares branches as flaming droplets
copper and bronze, fall

to gutters, sidewalks, spread hissing,
crackling to lawns, smolder until raked,
extinguished in bags brown, yellow, black.

Cost-Benefit Analysis: Spring 2020

Kim Sosin

Today I heard that, for the first time
in the memory of anyone alive,
Mount Everest is visible from Kathmandu.

Today I heard that, for the first time
in the memory of anyone alive,
dolphins swam in the clear waters of Venice.

Today I heard that we can see stars
through clear air over Beijing, LA, and DC.

Today I heard that NASA's satellites reveal
higher air quality over all major airports.

Today I heard that carbon emissions dropped,
slowing global climate change.

Today I heard that, for the first time,
a friend saw an Indigo Bunting in her yard.

Today I heard the unimaginable cost,
over 300,000 human souls.

Minimum Maintenance Roads

Kim Sosin

With my oldest but still younger brother beside me
I'm driving our parents' 1960 green Ford V8
crunching down tracks of crushed red gravel.
The engine pulls a train of billowing orange dust
on a new route between our small-town home
    and country church.

Our parents seldom left town, but for us, this,
our little frisson of travel in deserted places.
He spies the sign: "minimum maintenance road,"
twin slashes in the dirt through a narrow opening.
"I wonder what's down those tracks?"
My brother and I did not, probably could not,
since the day we started to drive without parents,
    resist that temptation.

The more messy-scary-hair-raising the voyage
    the greater the adventure.
We've dropped into sloppy mudholes,
    "Gun it," he hollers.
We've driven in tracks on an unstable rock ledge,
alternating dirty words with sort-of prayers
    "Oh crap! Oh my God!"
We've slammed the brakes, both screaming "stop,"
our front tires skidding onto a wood bridge,
    yawning missing boards.

Success meant not getting trapped, stuck, hurt,
    not being forced to back out.
I wish we could explore again, my brother and I,
with a rekindled sense of teenager immortality.
To look down a lane of two suspicious dirt gashes,
    "I wonder what's down that road?"
And off we'd go, a quest
    for somebody's once was.

Our River, Our Dance

Kim Sosin

A shaft of dawn sunlight dances
up the waking river,
the breeze stroking long white feathers.
The crane spreads wings to catch morning fire,
leaps, soars in wonder for the new day.

I know why I braved the uneven walk in cornstalks
stumbled through darkness, endured the cold wait
stood in the old photo blind until early light.
He spins, shimmies, struts, sways. Dance!
We burst with morning's joy.

The Cutting

Nathan Sousek

Rain is like a thrown knife.

Beautiful, sharp to the eye—it'll mesmerize
and mangle, split you down the middle
if you give it long enough.

He would stare out the windows on days like those,
when the rain would fall, at times as a silver sheet of liquid steel,
at others, a tickling mist which the trees kept shaking off.
He'd watch out that window saying if only it quit raining,
he'd go out and get something done.
This, the man who'd simultaneously curse and pray for rain
    when the summer sun
set the crops steaming like the cup of coffee in his hands on
    either day. But he'd
never say which he preferred more—the rain, the heat, or the
    cup of coffee.

She spoke not a word.
She'd heard it before. All of it . . .
As he kept speaking aloud, she thought silently
and watched the rain from a different window.

Setting

Nathan Sousek

She perched there—
a scarlet portrait atop the wooden fence
demure, radiant and with all the naturalness
as if she were a bird perching amid the branches of a tree,
with all the facetious flair of fire. And so she was—a flame
burning before the cloud-dappled sky, shimmering in a cloak
of liquid light, a molten dress which sways like wind and honey.
Like a muse upon her stage, she moves, graceful, proud, and
    suggestive—
as if performance were her nature, her nature to pander to an
    audience;
a bash of eyes, a flash of tail, a roll of shoulders to send her
    liquid shroud
rippling once more. Clever is her beauty, untamed as the rain,
fleeting as snow in spring or vain as a blue jay's song.
And with the sun she sets off—a flame soon lost to the darkness.

Slow

Nathan Sousek

The words come slow
bubbling to the surface
like the sun on a cold
winter dawn. Suffice

it to say, they do not come
fast enough, do not rise
like spring tulips lifting from
the loam, but thaw as if through winter ice.

No, they come slow, as lightning
bugs wafting up from the ditch grass,
as a chick struggling against and fighting
out of its shell—as the last

light passing below the horizon
on Solstice Day in June.

The work is frustrating. I am impatient.
I long for the words to gush
forth from the hydrant,
not flow like the natural creek whose gentle rush-

-ing tarries, waiting to be watched, to be
heard, to be witnessed, understood.
To understand is to see—to see
the nature of words as you would

your breath on a frigid dawn, sharp
and effervescent. It's in this moment I know,
they come, as the night's crooning lark,
as a breath taken deep   and let out slow.

How to Find and Follow our Authors

Some of our authors share their work and writing lives online. Here's where you can find them.

Lin Marshall Brummels
    https://wordpress.com/view/llzranch.blog
    LinkedIn: https://www.linkedin.com/in/lin-brummels-23453a26/
    Twitter: @linbrummmels

Marilyn Coffey
    https://www.marilyncoffey.net

Grace Gugel
    Facebook: G St. Creative

Jen Ippensen
    https://www.jenippensen.com
    Twitter: @jippensen

Julie Paschold
    https://jpaschold.blogspot.com/
    https://medium.com/@jpaschold

Holly Pelesky
    https://hollypelesky.com
    Twitter: @hollypelesky

Charlene Pierce
    Twitter: @CharWithAPen
    Instagram: @CharWithAPen

Kim Sosin
 https://sosin.us

Shyla Shehan
 https://shylashehan.com/
 Twitter: @shyspark
 Shyla is also the managing editor for the online literary publication *The Good Life Review*. Check it out! https://thegoodlifereview.com/

Acknowledgments

Thank you to everyone who submitted poems for the collection. We received over 340 entries from 84 poets. Our evaluators were very busy!

Thank you to everyone who worked to make the collection a great success:

Project Coordinator: Charlene Pierce
Project Consultants: Kim Sosin, Lori Joseph, Brandy Prettyman
Submissions Clerk: Julie Haase
Evaluators: Sharon Carr, Charlene Neely, Tami Whitney, Becky Faber, Chad Christiansen
Cover Design: Kim Sosin
Interior Design and Formatting: Julie Haase
Proofreading: Teresa Burt, Kim Sosin

Finally, thank you to the Board of the Nebraska Writers Guild for supporting this project.

President: Charles Lieske
Vice-President: Victorine Lieske
Treasurer: Faith A. Colburn
Recording Secretary: Kim Stokely
Membership Coordinator: Sarah Burhman
Member-at-Large: Jennifer Hanisch

Index by Author

Baron, Susan 1
Baumel, Zoe 3
Biggs, D. S. 6
Bonet, J. Eleanor 9
brown, j. kirk 11, 14, 15, 16
Brummels, Lin Marshall 17, 18
Coffey, Marilyn June 20
Dorf, Marilyn 21, 22, 24, 25, 26
Faber, Becky 27
Gugel, Grace 29
Harrison, Neil 31
Holmes, Bryant 32
Ippensen, Jen 35
Kopuri, Sreekanth 36, 39
Lester, Karla 40
Lucas, Scott L. 42
Luebbe, James 43, 44, 45, 46, 48, 49
Mason, Clif 50
McEvoy, Lillian 51
Mier, Guadalupe J. 52
Moran, Ricardo 54
Neely, Charlene 56
Paschold, Julie S. 59, 61
Pelesky, Holly 63
Petelle, John 65, 66

Pierce, Charlene 68
Shehan, Shyla 70
Smith, Rachel E. 72, 74, 75, 76
Sosin, Kim 77, 78, 80
Sousek, Nathan 81, 82, 83

Index by Title

Alive and Berried/Ripe for the Picking 6
Alive Here 9
Before Renovation 17
Black Horse, Red Truck, Old Man 11
Cost-Benefit Analysis: Spring 2020 77
Cutting, The 81
Day at Auschwitz, A 36
Death by Indifference 14
Death of George Floyd 40
Die-Cast Car 43
Earth Hunger 72
Easter in the Wood 15
Elderly Gardener 16
Emergency Room Breakfast 22
Encounter 20
Family Secret 44
Four O Two 51
Fuel 74
Green Leaves 1
Herdin' Wild Pink Rabbits 56
How to Growl 63
Howling at the Moon with My Mother 75
I Was Her and She Was Me 29
In the Absence of Memory 27
In the Morning 32
Inferno 76
Jackalope 46
Losing the Body 50

Loss 59
Mean Little Girl, Across Town 45
Minimum Maintenance Roads 78
Mother's Needlework 21
Natural Habitat 68
Our River, Our Dance 80
Parts Poem 48
Pastels in Grayscale 66
Peas 61
Princess in Exile, A 3
Priorities 65
Reason for Darkness, The 24
Reported Missing 18
Road Trip 54
Setting 82
Slow 83
Speed of the Valley 70
State of the Union 31
Takeoff, The 42
Talk That Takes Us Far, The 49
Tomorrow 39
Tree Talks Trash, The (a poem for Arbor Day) 52
What Poetry Is 25
When Night Comes 35
Who Can Say 26

www.ingramcontent.com/pod-product-compliance
Lightning Source LLC
Chambersburg PA
CBHW020913080526
44589CB00011B/572